CHARLIE BROWN'S CYCLOPEDIA

PLANES AND THINGS THAT FLY
Up, Up, And Away

VOLUME · 15 ·

Based on the Charles M. Schulz Characters
Funk & Wagnalls

Charlie Brown's 'Cyclopedia
has been produced
by Mega-Books of New York,
Inc. in conjunction
with the editorial, design,
and marketing staff of
Field Publications.

STAFF FOR
MEGA-BOOKS

Pat Fortunato
Editorial Director

Diana Papasergiou
Production Director

Susan Lurie
Executive Editor

Rosalind Noonan
Senior Editor

Adam Schmetterer
Research Director

**Michaelis/Carpelis
Design Assoc., Inc.**
Art Direction and Design

STAFF FOR
FIELD PUBLICATIONS

Cathryn Clark Girard
Assistant Vice President,
Juvenile Publishing

Elizabeth Isele
Executive Editor

Kristina Jones
Executive Art Director

Leslie Erskine
Marketing Manager

Elizabeth Zuraw
Senior Editor

Michele Italiano-Perla
Group Art Director

Kathleen Hughes
Senior Art Director

Photograph and Illustration Credits:
Courtesy of the Air Force Thunderbirds, 45; Craig Aurness/West Light, 54; The Bettmann Archive, 22, 23, 24, 25, 28, 42, 46; © 1989 Bill Crump, The Confederate Air Force, 44; Defense Image, 48; Michael Dick/Earth Scenes, 13; Kenneth Garrett/West Light, 27; General Dynamics, 47; The Granger Collection, 15, 51; Mark Greenberg/Visions, 57; B.E. Johnson/Discover Magazine, 58; Larry Lee/West Light, 38, 51; Howard Levy, 40, 41, 42, 43, 56; McDonnell Douglas Corp., 48; © 1989 Metroplitan Life Insurance Company, NY, NY, 20; Courtesy of Moller International, 59; Nick Nicholson/Image Bank, 17; Chuck O'Rear/West Light, 55; Ralph A. Reinhold/Earth Scenes, 52; © 1971 Ripley Entertainment, Inc., 12; Lucille Sardegna/West Light, 53; Steve Strickland/West Light, 36; Dick Thorn, 13, 22, 28; UPI/Bettmann Newsphotos, 19, 26, 35; All Sport Vandystadt/West Light, 60; Ron Watts/West Light, 32; West Light, 30; PH 1 Jeffrey Wood/The Blue Angels, 33.

ISBN: 0-8374-0062-7

Part of the material in this volume was previously published in *Charlie Brown's Second Super Book of Questions and Answers*.

Funk & Wagnalls, founded in 1876, is the publisher of *Funk & Wagnalls New Encyclopedia*, one of the most widely owned home and school reference sets, and many other adult and juvenile educational publications.

INTRODUCTION

Welcome to volume 15 of *Charlie Brown's 'Cyclopedia!* Have you ever wondered when people first tried to fly, or who the Red Baron really was? Charlie Brown and the rest of the *Peanuts* gang are here to help you find the answers to these questions and many more about planes and other things that fly. Have fun!

CONTENTS

Long ago, people tried all sorts of ways to fly like the birds. It wasn't until hot-air balloons were invented, though, that people finally got off the ground safely. Let's climb aboard Linus's balloon and travel back through time to see how people first began to reach for the sky.

UP, UP, AND AWAY

GETTING OFF THE GROUND

How did people first try to fly?

People made wings of feathers and tried to fly like birds. They attached their homemade wings to their arms and jumped from high places. Usually, they were killed or badly injured.

In 1490, an Italian named Danti made some wings to help him fly. For a moment, it looked as if they would work, but Danti crashed to the ground.

In about 1500, a man named Wan Ho tried to fly in China. He tied 47 rockets to the back of his chair. Then he strapped himself in. His friends attached two kites to his chair, then lit the rockets. There was a big explosion. Wan Ho was never seen again.

© 1971 Ripley Entertainment, Inc.
Registered Trademark of
Ripley Entertainment, Inc.

IN 1742 THE MARQUIS de BACQUEVILLE BROKE BOTH OF HIS LEGS TRYING TO *FLY* ACROSS THE SEINE RIVER in France *WITH GIANT WINGS TIED TO HIS HANDS AND FEET!*

BALLOONS

What was the first successful flying machine?

The first successful flying machine was a balloon built by Joseph and Jacques Montgolfier (ZHOCK mawn-gawl-FYAY) in 1782. One day, while watching a fire in their fireplace, the brothers noticed that the smoke went up the chimney. The brothers wondered why. When Joseph and Jacques trapped some smoke in a paper bag, the bag floated in the air.

Later that year, they took a bag that measured 35 feet around and weighed 300 pounds. The brothers made a smoky fire and floated the bag over the fire. It rose more than a mile high before it cooled off and came back down. This was the first balloon flight. Later, people discovered that it was hot air and not smoke that made balloons rise.

A propane heater is used to heat air to inflate this balloon.

BALLOON RISES

BALLOON DESCENDS

When air is heated, cold air is forced out.

When burner is turned off, cool air rushes in.

Burner

Basket

How does the hot-air balloon work?

A hot-air balloon is a large, airtight cloth or plastic bag that is open at the bottom. The balloon is filled with heated air. Hot air is lighter than cool air, so hot air rises. The hot air inside the balloon is lighter than the cool air outside, so the balloon rises. When the heated air cools and becomes as heavy as the air outside, the balloon will stop rising and come down.

A hot-air balloon carries people in a basket attached to its bottom end. Hot-air balloons also carry propane heaters to heat air. A blast from the heater causes the balloon to rise higher. When the passengers want to come down, they can open the top of the balloon to let out heated air.

13

Who was the first person to fly?

Pilatre de Rozier (pee-LAH-truh DUH row-ZYAY) of France was the first person to fly. A duck, a sheep, and a rooster had already flown in a Montgolfier balloon. Now it was a person's turn. King Louis XVI (the six-teenth) offered to send up a prisoner who was to be executed soon, but de Rozier begged to go.

On October 15, 1783, de Rozier climbed aboard the balloon. It rose 80 feet into the air, about as high as a six-story building. It proba-bly would have gone higher, but it was held down by a rope. Man's first flight lasted four and a half minutes.

Early balloons carried sponges and a bucket of water for putting out the fires that kept starting!

YOU FLY IN A BALLOON? YOU CAN'T EVEN FLY A KITE, BIG BROTHER!

In 1870, a man named Leon Gambetta used a hot-air balloon to escape from Paris, France, when Germany was attacking the city.

How did people first use balloons?

After de Rozier's first balloon flight, people tried to see how far they could go in balloons. A Frenchman, Jean Pierre Blanchard (ZHON PYAIR blon-SHAR), crossed the English Channel in a balloon in 1785. A balloon called the *Great Balloon of Nassau* sailed 500 miles, from London, England, to Germany in 1836. Balloons were also used in World War I and other wars to observe enemy armies.

How fast can a balloon go?

A balloon has no moving power of its own. It can travel only as fast as the wind that carries it.

POOF! POOF! POOF!

Why did people stop using balloons for travel?

Balloon flight can't be controlled. Some people tried to steer balloons by using sails. Others tried oars. A few people tried paddles. Nothing worked. When better airships were invented, people lost interest in balloons.

How are balloons used today?

Scientists use very big plastic balloons to gather weather information. These balloons carry equipment to record temperature, humidity (moisture), air pressure, and wind speeds. This information is sent back to the scientists by radio equipment, which is also carried by the balloons.

If a weather balloon breaks, the instruments it carries float back to the Earth in a bright red parachute.

How else are balloons used?

Today, people travel in balloons as a sport. Balloon races were held in the United States as early as 1906, and today, balloonists still participate in races and contests for fun. Many races, such as the Albuquerque Balloon Fiesta in New Mexico, aren't really competitive races. They are more like festivals, where people gather to enjoy watching or riding in the brightly-colored balloons. Races or festivals are usually held in a place where there is a lot of wide, open space. Sometimes as many as 500 balloons lift off in succession!

No, it's not a plane. It's a balloon built to resemble one!

What do today's balloons look like?

Today's balloons come in many different shapes. Some are still round, like the first balloon built by the Montgolfier brothers. Others, like some you might see at a balloon festival, resemble cartoon characters or everyday objects. There are balloons shaped like Donald Duck's head, a hamburger, and even a cow jumping over a moon!

DIRIGIBLES

What first replaced the balloon?

The dirigible (DIR-ih-juh-bull), also called an airship, first replaced the balloon. Like a balloon, a dirigible is wingless and weighs less than air. Unlike a balloon, it has a propeller and an engine and can be steered with a rudder. The rudder is a movable part at the rear of a dirigible. When the pilot moves the rudder to the right, the front of the airship moves right. When the rudder is moved left, the front of the airship moves left.

A rubberlike skin fits over a rigid frame in most dirigibles. The skin is filled with gas that weighs less than air. The gas inside the dirigible gives the airship its shape. A dirigible usually looks like a giant cigar. The first successful dirigible was flown in 1852. It had a top speed of six miles an hour. That's about as fast as a brisk roller-skate ride.

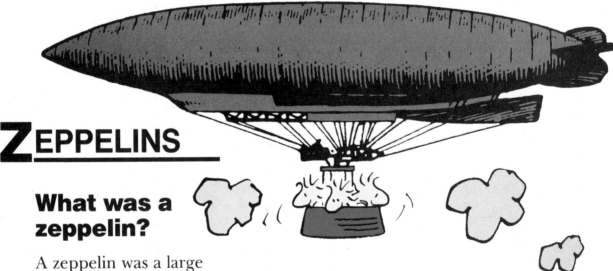

ZEPPELINS

What was a zeppelin?

A zeppelin was a large dirigible. It was named for the man who designed it, Count Ferdinand von Zeppelin of Germany.

The first zeppelin was built in 1900. It had a cigar-shaped aluminum frame and weighed 25,350 pounds, about as much as three elephants.

How were zeppelins used?

Zeppelins carried passengers who wanted to go sightseeing. Regularly scheduled zeppelin flights were made across the Atlantic Ocean. Count von Zeppelin began an airship company that carried 34,288 people in four years without an accident. During World War I, zeppelins had another use. The Germans built 100 zeppelins for military use. Their mission: bombing London!

In 1928, ten years after World War I, the Graf Zeppelin, a large German zeppelin, flew around the world in 22 days!

What was the *Hindenburg*?

The *Hindenburg* was the largest airship ever built. It was a zeppelin 803 feet long. That's about as long as 54 cars in a line. The *Hindenburg* was 135 feet wide—about as wide as 9 cars in a line. The *Hindenburg* had a lounge, a piano, and paneled bedrooms. It made 35 trips across the Atlantic Ocean. On May 6, 1937, it suddenly exploded and burned as it was trying to land at Lakehurst, New Jersey. There were 97 people aboard. Thirty-six of them died. No one ever found out what caused the disaster, but zeppelins were filled with hydrogen gas, which people knew was very explosive. After the *Hindenburg* tragedy, hydrogen was never used in airships again, and zeppelins were never again manufactured.

The *Hindenburg* exploded on May 6, 1937.

Will zeppelins ever be used again?

Perhaps zeppelins will be used again in the future. Scientists today are beginning to think about lighter-than-air aircraft once again. A zeppelin, if powered by the most powerful energy in the world—atomic energy—might work well. Because atomic energy uses very little fuel, an atomic zeppelin would not have to be refueled very often. It could remain in the air for a week at a time. A zeppelin can stay still in the sky, so it could remain in one place while scientists studied the land and water below. The U.S. military wants to use zeppelins to patrol borders. Some people are sure that zeppelins will make a comeback.

BLIMPS

Snoopy is everywhere— even on a blimp!

© 1989 Metropolitan Life Insurance Company, NY, NY

I ATE THE WHOLE BAG, AND NOW I FEEL LIKE A BLIMP!

Are blimps the same as zeppelins?

Blimps are small dirigibles. They are usually filled with helium gas. No one is sure how the blimp got its nickname. The first model was called an A-limp. The B-limp was the improved version. Some say that B-limp was shortened to blimp. Others say the name came from the sound of a thumb thumping the blimp during the preflight check. If it sounded like "blimp," the inflation was correct. The few blimps around today are used for advertising.

CHAPTER 2

Famous pilots have often become heroes around the world. Their sense of adventure and daredevil stunts have thrilled people in all corners of the Earth. What's that in the sky? Why, it's Woodstock, asking you to come along and meet some famous firsts in flight!

FAMOUS FLIERS

THE WRIGHT BROTHERS

Orville and Wilbur Wright

Who invented the airplane?

The Wright brothers invented the first safe, successful airplane. However, their first flight, near Kitty Hawk, North Carolina, didn't make great news. Nothing appeared in the newspapers on that day—December 17, 1903. A few days later, short items began to appear in newspapers across the country, but no one seemed very interested or impressed. Today, that flight is known around the world.

How long did the first airplane flight last?

Orville Wright took the *Flyer I* up in the air and flew it for 12 seconds. That same day, Wilbur Wright took turns with his brother flying their airplane. The next two flights lasted twice as long as the first one. On the fourth flight that day, the airplane stayed in the air for 59 seconds.

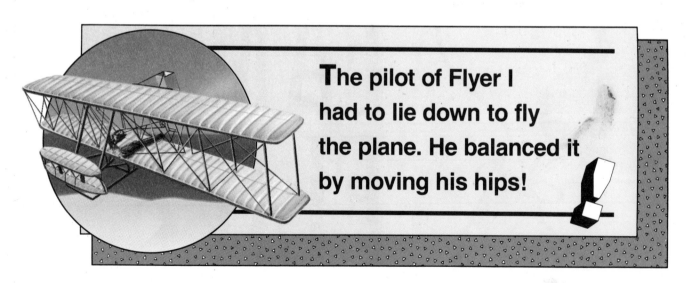

The pilot of Flyer I had to lie down to fly the plane. He balanced it by moving his hips!

What did the *Flyer I* look like?

The *Flyer I* was a biplane. That means it had two sets of wings, one above the other. The two propellers were behind the pilot. This kind of biplane was later called a pusher plane because the air flowed out the back, pushing the plane forward. In World War I, the propeller was moved to the front so that it "pulled" the plane.

Another Wright flyer—this one built by the brothers in 1908 at the request of the U.S. government.

The propellers on Flyer I were attached to the engine by a bicycle chain!

Flyer I

WITH A NAME LIKE WRIGHT, WHAT COULD BE WRONG?

23

FAMOUS FIRSTS

Who was the first person to fly across the sea?

Louis Blériot (loo-EE blay-RYO) flew across the English Channel from France to England in 1909. He showed that people from different countries could now visit each other fairly easily. Blériot received a reward for

Louis Blériot sits in the monoplane he flew across the English Channel.

his feat. When he completed the Channel crossing in his *Blériot XI* (eleven) monoplane, he won a prize of $5,000 from a British newspaper.

The Baroness de la Roche was the first woman pilot.

Who was the first woman pilot?

The Baroness de la Roche (DUH LAH RAWSH) was the first woman pilot. She made her first flight in 1908 without a pilot's license! Two years later, she was given one.

Who was the first person to cross the Atlantic Ocean?

The first crossing of the Atlantic Ocean was made in 1919 by a man named Albert C. Read. Four U.S. Navy seaplanes—NC-1, NC-2, NC-3, and NC-4— planned to make the journey. NC-4, Lieutenant Commander Read's plane, was the only one to make it. He and a five-man crew flew from Newfoundland in Canada to the Azores, which are islands in the middle of the Atlantic Ocean, and then on to Lisbon, Portugal.

When was the first nonstop flight made across the Atlantic?

Eighteen days later, two Englishmen named John Alcock and Arthur Brown flew nonstop from Newfoundland to Ireland. Their plane was a World War I military plane.

Wiley Post (left) and Harold Gatty (right) wave to cheering fans in New York City after completing the fastest trip around the world in 1931.

Who were the first men to circle around the world in a plane?

The U.S. Army Air Service sent out four planes in 1924. Two of them made it around the world. The pilots' names were Lowell Smith and Erik Nelson. The trip took 150 days.

Was 150 days the fastest trip at that time?

It wasn't even close to being the fastest. Zeppelins had made the trip around the world many years before planes did. The *Graf Zeppelin* made the trip in 21 days. Still, most airplane pilots knew they could break that record. In fact, in 1931, a pilot named Wiley Post and a navigator named Harold Gatty said they could do it in 10 days. Instead, they did it in 8 days, 15 hours, and 51 minutes.

FAMOUS FIRSTS

Who was the first person to fly solo, or alone, around the world?

Wiley Post did it again. Because Wiley did not have much education, people believed that he couldn't have made his first trip without Harold Gatty. This upset Wiley. He claimed he could make the trip by himself, and do it in 7 days. He did. He went around the world in 7 days, 18 hours, and 49 minutes.

LUCKY LINDY

Who was Lucky Lindy?

Lucky Lindy was the nickname of a man named Charles Lindbergh, one of the most famous fliers of all time. Even though he was the 79th person to cross the Atlantic, he was the first person to do it alone. Raymond Orteig, a New York City hotel owner, offered to give $25,000 to the first person to fly nonstop from New York to Paris. Charles Lindbergh accepted the challenge.

St. Louis businessmen paid for a plane, the *Spirit of St. Louis*, built specially for Lindbergh. Its cockpit was just the right size for his body, and it had five fuel tanks. To save space for fuel, Lindbergh didn't take even a parachute or radio.

When was Lindbergh's famous flight?

On May 20, 1927, Lindbergh took off early in the morning from Roosevelt Field in Garden City, New York. He flew his plane through fog, rain, and sleet. He hadn't slept the night before because he was so nervous, so he had to fight to stay awake on the long trip. He landed in Paris 33 hours and 30 minutes later. He had flown 3,600 miles.

Lindbergh brought along five sandwiches. Because he thought that food might put him to sleep, he ate only one and a half during the long trip!

How did Lindbergh start flying?

From almost the first time he saw a plane, Lindbergh knew that he wanted to fly. He started working as a stunt person with a barnstormer. He saved his money to buy a plane, then taught himself how to fly. For a while he worked as an airmail pilot.

What was barnstorming?

Barnstorming was a type of show that stunt pilots gave in the early days of airplanes. Barnstorming pilots flew their planes from one small town to another, stopping wherever a fair or festival was going on. Airplanes were an unusual sight then, so people gathered to watch. The pilot would swoop low over towns and nearby farms, and a stunt person accompanying the pilot would perform daring feats such as parachute jumps and walking on the plane's wings. When the plane landed, the pilot would sell short rides in it for about $5.

Tied to a plane by strong cables, a stunt person can fly standing up—and upside down!

What happened to the *Spirit of St. Louis*?

After Lindbergh made his famous flight to Paris, he and his plane were brought back on a Navy ship. Lindbergh now was a hero. After a tour of all 48 states, he gave his plane to a museum in Washington, D.C. You can still see the *Spirit of St. Louis* and many other famous planes at the Smithsonian National Air and Space Museum in Washington, D.C.

AMELIA EARHART

Who was Amelia Earhart?

Amelia Earhart was a famous pilot who achieved a lot of firsts. She was the first woman to receive the Distinguished Flying Cross award, and she was the first to fly alone across the United States in both directions. She was the first woman to cross the Atlantic as a passenger, and she was also the first woman (and second person) to cross it solo. Even though she made it across, she was forced to cut her flight short. When she was over Ireland, she noticed that her fuel tank was leaking. This forced her to land, but she did make it!

To prepare for her first long solo flight, Amelia Earhart practiced going without sleep or food for many days at a time. She didn't need all the practice. Her trip lasted only about 14 hours!

What finally happened to Amelia Earhart?

In 1937, she and her navigator, Fred Noonan, tried to fly a twin-engine airplane around the world. They didn't make it. A ship picked up a radio signal from their airplane. The plane was short of fuel over the Pacific Ocean. That was the last anyone heard from them. Planes and ships searched, but no trace of Amelia Earhart, Fred Noonan, or their plane was ever found.

CHAPTER 3

You hear the engines whirring. You see the silver jets soaring across the sky. How do those giant planes fly through the air? Fasten your seat belt, and Charlie Brown will take you on a trip through the clouds to show you all about flying.

FASTEN YOUR SEAT BELT

TAKING OFF

A big airplane has to gather a lot of speed before the lift force is strong enough to raise it off the ground.

How can a heavy plane stay up in the air?

When a plane is flying, it is being pulled up and down and backward and forward all at the same time. The force of gravity pulls the plane downward. Lift—the force made by the wings as they cut through the air— pushes it upward. The force of drag pulls the plane backward, while a force called thrust pushes it forward. Jet engines or propellers give thrust. A heavy plane in steady flight stays in the air for two reasons. The thrust from its engines or propellers equals the drag force, and the lift made by its wings equals the force of gravity on the plane (its weight).

What are runways used for?

An airplane needs a runway to take off and to land. An airplane must race across the ground to gather speed before the lift force is strong enough to raise it off the ground.

Small planes can leave the ground at speeds of only 30 to 40 miles an hour. That is slower than cars normally travel on a highway. Heavier planes may have to reach 100 miles an hour before they can lift into the air. That is almost twice the speed limit for cars on a highway.

Are runways used for anything else?

Runways are also used for landings. In a car, a driver has to start braking a good distance before actually stopping. The faster the car is going, the longer the distance has to be. If a driver brakes quickly, the car will jerk and everyone will be thrown forward. The same is true of planes. Pilots need long runways so that they can brake slowly and give the passengers a comfortable stop.

PARTS OF AN AIRPLANE

What are the most important parts of an airplane?

Modern airplanes have three main parts. They are the wings, the tail assembly, and the body. The body is called the fuselage (FYOO-suh-lahj).

How are the wings important?

The airplane's wings provide lift to push the plane into the sky. As long as the engines are providing thrust and speed at the same time, the airplane can stay up.

What is the tail assembly?

The tail assembly keeps the plane steady. It is made up of three parts: the rudder, the fin, and the stabilizer. The pilot swings the rudder to the right to move the plane right or to the left to move the plane left. The fin is the part of the tail assembly that keeps the plane steady in forward flight. The stabilizer keeps the airplane from wobbling up and down. Other tail parts called elevators are connected to the stabilizer. They help the plane go up and down during takeoffs and landings.

Why is the fuselage important?

This is where the passengers sit or where freight is stored. The fuselage also includes the cockpit, the place where the pilot sits. All the plane's controls are in the cockpit.

What are ailerons?

Ailerons (AY-luh-ronz) are movable flaps on the wings that let the pilot tilt the plane left or right. This is called banking. By banking the plane, the pilot makes it turn one way or the other. Other wing flaps give the plane stronger lift at the slower speeds of takeoff and landing.

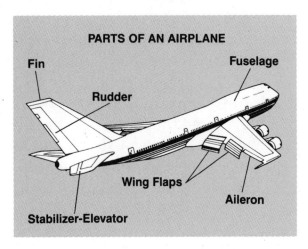

PARTS OF AN AIRPLANE

Fin

Rudder

Fuselage

Wing Flaps

Aileron

Stabilizer-Elevator

BECOMING A PILOT

How can you become a pilot?

Every pilot must have a license in order to fly an airplane. A person must be at least 16 years old to get a student's license, and 17 years old to get a regular license. Flying lessons are necessary, and they are expensive, too. Some people get their pilot's license by joining the armed forces, which has pilot training programs. Many colleges offer flight training programs. There are many things to learn about flying. Students usually take courses in weather, air science, and the rules of flying. A student pilot must spend at least 40 hours flying, first with a licensed instructor and then alone. The student must complete one 300-mile flight without having the instructor in the plane. Then the student takes a flight test, or check ride, with a licensed examiner on board. A pilot must also pass a written test and a physical examination by a doctor.

Every part of the plane must be checked before takeoff.

FLYING A PLANE

What happens to a plane before it is ready to take off?

An airplane is thoroughly checked by the airplane's safety crew before it is allowed to leave the airport. A person from the Federal Aviation Administration spotchecks the plane to be sure it is safe. Everything in the airplane must be working correctly. Mechanics who work on it are well trained. They know how to take an engine completely apart. They can put it together again so that it runs perfectly. A safety person checks the weight of the baggage, the passengers, and the cargo. The dispatcher decides the route the pilot will take and how high he or she should fly. The weather station tells the pilot what the weather conditions will be like during the flight.

The pilot and the flight crew check the instruments on the control panel. They use a checklist. The pilot names an instrument, and the copilot or flight engineer checks the instrument to be sure it is working right.

What happens when the plane is all set to go?

The pilot starts the engines. He or she speaks to the control tower by radio. The control tower tells the pilot which runway to use. The pilot taxis to the runway. Once the control tower gives clearance, the plane rolls down the runway. Then the pilot raises the nose and steers the plane into lift-off.

How can a plane fly upside down?

A plane can fly upside down because the same forces—lift, drag, thrust, and gravity— that pull on a right-side-up plane also pull on an upside-down plane. The only force that may not be strong in an upside-down plane is lift—the force made by the wings as they cut through the air. As long as the wings have enough lift in the

U.S. Navy fliers called the Blue Angels perform amazing feats in the air.

upside-down position, the plane will stay in the air. First, however, the ailerons—the movable flaps near the tips of the wings—must turn the plane over. By moving the ailerons, the pilot can roll the plane over.

What is an automatic pilot?

An automatic pilot is a set of instruments that flies the plane without any help from the human pilot. The automatic pilot can keep the plane flying in the right direction. It can keep it at the correct height in the sky. The automatic pilot can be more precise than a human pilot.

If the weather is bad and rain, snow, or fog blocks the view, the pilot may use the automatic pilot. Pilots also use it if they are busy doing something else. Someday, flight may become completely automatic. Perhaps computers, not people, will guide airplanes throughout an entire flight.

CHAPTER 4

Planes have become quite common. People no longer run out of their houses to look when a plane flies overhead, as they did in the early days of airplane flight. Even though seeing a plane is not an unusual event, planes are very important. Without them, life as we know it today would be very different. Here are some of the ways that planes at work help us.

PLANES AT WORK

AIRMAIL

When did people start using airplanes to deliver the mail?

Some early airplane pilots and balloonists carried mail as a stunt, but the first official United States airmail delivery was made in 1911. That flight was made by Paul Beck and Earle Ovington, who delivered mail from Garden City, New York, to Jamaica, New York, a distance of less than eight miles.

Earle Ovington was the pilot of the first U.S. airmail flight in 1911.

Today, almost all mail that travels more than 100 miles goes by air!

HOW NICE... AN AIRMAIL LETTER!

When did airmail really become part of the post office delivery system?

May 15, 1917, was the beginning of the first continuous airmail service in the world. Army pilots flew military mail from cities in Europe to New York City, Philadelphia, and Washington, D.C. Regular airmail service from the United States to Europe began in 1918. People paid much more to send a letter by air. Otherwise, the mail would go by boat, a much slower way of delivery.

BUSH PILOTS

What do bush pilots do?

Bush pilots fly to areas where very few people live. These areas are usually on mountains or in jungles or near the North and South poles. Bush pilots deliver food, medicine, and supplies. They take sick people to hospitals. There aren't as many bush pilots today as there used to be because there aren't as many isolated places.

Is bush piloting dangerous?

Often it is. Winds near the poles may gust up to 100 miles per hour. Isolated areas usually don't have weather stations, so a pilot has to judge the weather himself. Some places don't have airports or landing strips. A pilot might have to land in a field or even on ice. If the ice is too thin, the pilot is in serious danger.

A "crop duster" sprays chemicals over a field of crops.

PLANES FOR FARMERS AND FIRE FIGHTERS

How do planes help farmers?

Farmers need to spray their crops with chemicals to protect them from insect pests. The easiest way to do this is by plane. Farmers hire special planes that have big storage tanks to hold the chemicals. The plane flies low over the fields and sprays the chemicals on the crops.

How do planes fight fires?

Fire-fighting planes are like the planes farmers use to spray their crops. A fire-fighting plane has a storage area that can be unloaded over the fire. This storage area holds fire-fighting chemicals or water.

There is a Canadian plane that can suck up water from a lake! The water is then released over a fire.

PICTURES FROM THE SKY

How do photographers use planes?

There are many uses for aerial pictures—pictures taken from the air. Many travel brochures use aerial pictures. That is a good way to show all of a resort or even an entire country. The military takes aerial pictures of countries they believe are a threat. Such pictures locate the air and military bases of a possible enemy. Military technicians can study the pictures.

Pictures are good for mapmaking, too. An aerial photograph is almost a map all by itself. A mapmaker just copies what he or she sees and adds the right marks and names. Before planes were used in mapmaking, it was much more difficult to figure out exactly what a place looked like.

YOUR TURN TO FLY

WAIT! DON'T LEAVE WITHOUT ME!

What is a scheduled airline?

Scheduled airlines fly planes every day at regular times. They are the ones who use the 400 biggest airports. There are about 13,000 airports in the United States. Almost 5,000 of these are public airports. Another 739 private airports are available for public use.

Are there any other airports?

Yes. There are private airports that can be used only by the members of the club or organization that owns the airport. The armed forces have more than 400 airports, which are open only to people in the military. Some military airports are used for transporting people and equipment, and others are used for trying out new planes.

One of the world's busiest airports is the Atlanta International Airport. During 1987, a plane took off from there every 40 seconds!

CHAPTER · 5

Planes are extremely important to the armed forces. Some planes carry tanks and soldiers. Fighter planes attack other airplanes. Many new plane designs and ideas came about, unfortunately, because of war. Countries at war wanted the newest weapons to defend themselves.

SKY PATROL

IN THE BEGINNING

When were planes first used in a war?

Airplanes were first used for war in October 1911. During a war between Italy and Turkey, an Italian pilot flew over enemy lands to see what the people were doing there. Then the Italians decided they could use the planes to drop bombs. A few days later, another Italian pilot dropped four grenades over Turkey. He also scattered leaflets that urged the people to surrender.

WORLD WAR I PLANES

How were planes used in World War I?

In World War I, which took place from 1914 to 1918, some planes were used for observation. The Allied and the Central forces used the planes to spy on each other. The Allied forces were made up of Great Britain, France, Russia, Italy, and the United States. Germany, Austria-Hungary, Turkey, and Bulgaria made up the Central powers.

Each plane carried two people—a pilot and an observer. The observer made notes on enemy troops. Neither side wanted enemy planes to spy on them, so the observers started carrying rifles to shoot at other enemy planes.

This is a model of the Fokker Eindecker, which you can actually build from a kit!

What was the first true fighter plane?

A Dutchman named Anthony Fokker designed planes for the Germans. He solved an important military plane problem. The first machine guns put on planes would shoot holes in the planes' propellers. Fokker solved this problem by linking the gun and the plane's engine. Because of his idea, the gunfire missed the propeller every time. This plane was called the Fokker Eindecker, and it was the first true fighter plane.

The Spad was one of the fastest and strongest planes in World War I.

What were some of the other World War I planes?

A French plane called the Spad was the most popular. There were more Spads in World War I than any other plane. The Spad was very fast and strong. Another French plane was the Voisin. The Voisin was a plane that had a cannon mounted on the front and a gun mounted on the right-hand side of the cockpit.

What is a flying ace?

The term *flying ace* comes from World War I. An ace was any fighter pilot who shot down five or more enemy planes.

Here's a photo of the type of plane the Red Baron flew.

Who was the Red Baron?

The Red Baron of Germany was one of the greatest flying aces of all times. His real name was Baron Manfred von Richthofen (RIKHT-hoe-fun). He shot down 80 planes during World War I. The Allied ace who came closest was a Frenchman named Paul-René Fonck who shot down 75 planes. Richthofen was called the Red Baron because his plane was painted bright red. Baron von Richthofen was killed on April 21, 1918.

The Red Baron wasn't always a great pilot. On his first solo flight, he had to make a crash landing!

THE RED BARON JUST CALLED TO SAY HE CAN'T COME TODAY TO DESTROY YOU... BUT HE'S SENDING OVER HIS ASSISTANT...

© 1989 United Feature Syndicate. Inc

10-7

THE PINK BARON!

What are dogfights?

Dogfights are airplane battles in the sky. They were common during World War I, when squadrons of 10 to 20 planes fought each other in the sky. The planes twisted and turned in many directions as each pilot tried to shoot the enemy. A pilot would try to get behind an enemy plane before firing his guns. This kept him safe from bullets, but close enough to hit the enemy.

WORLD WAR II PLANES OF GERMANY, JAPAN, AND THE ALLIES

How were planes used in World War II?

More planes were made and used during World War II than at any other time. The war, fought from 1939 to 1945, was between the Allied and the Axis powers. The main Allied powers were the United States, Great Britain, and the Soviet Union. Germany, Italy, and Japan were the Axis powers. Germany's plan was to have many planes fly over and bomb enemy countries. Then, the army would finish the fight. They called this the Blitzkrieg, meaning "lightning war."

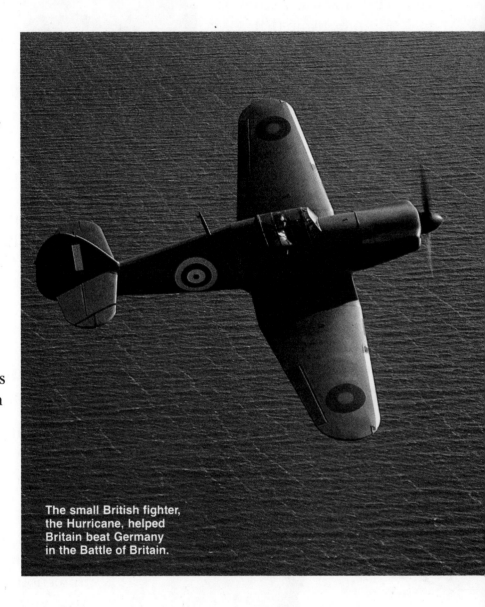

The small British fighter, the Hurricane, helped Britain beat Germany in the Battle of Britain.

What were some of the World War II planes?

The Stuka was a small German dive bomber. It was the star of the Blitzkrieg. It dropped heavy bombs one at a time and hit more Allied ships than any other plane. German bomber planes were clobbered in the Battle of Britain by small British fighters called Hurricanes and Spitfires. These planes were very fast and could spin and turn easily.

What was the Japanese Zero like?

Weighing in at more than 6,000 pounds, the Japanese Zero was actually a lightweight—for a plane, that is!

The Japanese Zero was a fighter plane that didn't have much power and wasn't very well protected. However, like the Hurricane, it could climb and turn very well. The heaviest model weighed only 6,025 pounds—about one-half the weight of U.S. Navy fighters. The Zero could reach speeds of 350 miles per hour. This was 20 miles per hour faster than any U.S. plane at the time. Some of the Japanese Zeros were flown by pilots called kamikazes.

Japanese kamikazes wanted to die for their country. When Japan started losing the war, kamikazes steered their planes into the decks of ships. The pilot would die, but the plane and its bomb damaged the enemy's ship.

I NEVER GO ON A MISSION WITHOUT MY BLANKET.

What planes were used against Japan?

One Allied plane that fought against the Zero was a Navy fighter called a Hellcat. With six machine guns and an engine that could deliver 2,000 horsepower, the Hellcat was a strong opponent for the Japanese Zero. Heavy armor plating gave the Hellcat protection against the Zero's two machine guns and two cannons.

Another Allied plane, the Boeing B-29 Superfortress, was the best bomber in World War II. The B-29 could carry 20,000 pounds of bombs and had ten remote-controlled machine guns. This was the type of plane that dropped nuclear bombs.

JET PLANES IN THE MODERN MILITARY

What is a jet plane?

A jet plane is an aircraft that has jet engines. When fuel is burned in a jet engine, it gives off hot gases. The gases shoot out of the back of the engine in a stream called a jet. The stream rushing out toward the rear makes the plane move in the forward motion we call thrust. Think of a toy balloon filled with air. If you suddenly let go of the stem, the balloon will zip away. Air rushes from the stem in one direction, pushing the balloon in the other direction—just like the jet plane.

How fast can a jet plane go?

One jet reached a speed of more than 2,193 miles per hour, but most jets can't go that fast. Most passenger jets travel at about 570 miles per hour.

What planes have been made since World War II?

Many planes have been built since World War II. In the Korean War, the North Koreans had Soviet MiGs, and the Allied forces had Sabres. These new jet fighters had sleek, modern designs. Jet bombers were made shortly after that. New planes were being invented more rapidly than ever. Soon, planes were going faster than the speed of sound. At sea level, the speed of sound is usually estimated to be 735 to 750 miles an hour. Because air density varies at different altitudes, the speed of sound varies.

Chuck Yeager stands next to Glamorous Glennis, the plane in which he broke the sound barrier.

Who was Chuck Yeager?

Charles "Chuck" Yeager, an Air Force pilot, was the first person to travel faster than the speed of sound. On October 14, 1947, he flew an X-1 rocket plane at 670 miles per hour, or Mach 1.015. The word *Mach* is a measurement of air speed. Mach 1 equals the speed of sound.

Because no one had ever broken the sound barrier, many people were afraid that dangerous things would happen to the pilot who attempted to do so. Some thought that any plane that tried to fly so fast would break apart. Others thought that the instrument controls wouldn't work. Yeager was willing to risk these dangers. His bravery paved the way for the supersonic flights of today.

Yeager's plane, the *Glamorous Glennis*, hangs in the National Air and Space Museum, by the Wright brothers' *Flyer I* and the *Apollo II* spacecraft.

HERE'S ANOTHER NEW MODEL, READY FOR FLIGHT!

What is the B-52 Stratofortress?

A giant jet bomber called the B-52 first flew in 1952. It was later used in the Vietnam War in the 1960s to drop as many as 100 bombs at a time. The B-52 flies at 400 miles per hour and is the oldest jet bomber still flying.

What is the F-16?

As planes got bigger and bigger, they became more expensive as well. Working for the U.S. Government, one company designed a smaller jet, called the F-16 Falcon. This plane is so fast, it can reach Mach 2 and it has only one engine! The plane uses a computer to help the pilot fly the aircraft. Plans for future F-16s include using a voice-activated computer that will allow the pilot simply to tell the plane what to do.

A pilot guides the super-fast F-16 into a turn.

What is the Stealth bomber?

The Stealth bomber is a U.S. military plane with a special advantage—it cannot be detected by radar. Its flat, smooth design, as well as materials that absorb radar, help to weaken radar signals. Instead, fuzzy or tiny signals are sent back to the enemy. Such weak signals are hard for the enemy to identify. The Stealth bomber can be used for secret spy missions or bombing raids because the enemy can't detect it.

STEALTH BOMBER

After taking off without a runway, the Harrier keeps climbing straight up into the sky.

What is the Harrier jet fighter?

The Harrier is a military jet with some special abilities. The Harrier can take off and land straight up and down without using a runway. This makes the Harrier valuable for fighting and transporting in areas that don't have runways or long flat spaces of land. The plane can hover, or stay in the air without moving, and can fly at almost the speed of sound. It can also carry more than 9,000 pounds of weapons!

CHAPTER 6

What's that strange thing zooming overhead? Can you name that plane? From helicopters to a triangle-shaped plane, the sky is filled with all kinds of machines!

NAME THAT PLANE!

PROP PLANES

What is a prop plane?

The *prop* in *prop plane* is short for propeller. Prop planes have propeller engines rather than jet engines. A prop plane has blades in the front that spin around. These blades make up the propeller. The propeller helps to move the airplane forward.

CHOP
CHOP
CHOP
CHOP

How fast can a prop plane fly?

The speed of a prop plane depends on the size of the plane and how many engines it has. The single-engine six-passenger Piper Malibu Mirage, a popular prop plane for private use, has a top speed of 300 miles per hour. Pilot Lyle Shelton holds the prop plane record at 528 miles per hour.

HELICOPTERS

Are the blades on a helicopter called propellers?

No. Helicopters have rotor blades. These rotor blades are like wings that spin around on top of the helicopter. By spinning very fast, they pull the helicopter up in the same way that wings lift a plane. By tilting the blades, the pilot can move the helicopter forward or backward. If the pilot doesn't tilt the blades at all, the helicopter can stay in one place.

Because a helicopter can go straight up and down, it doesn't need a runway. A helicopter can even land on the roof of a building!

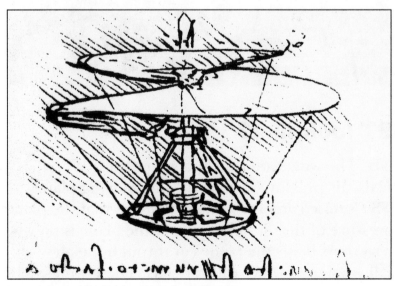

Who invented the helicopter?

About 500 years ago, a famous artist and inventor named Leonardo da Vinci (lay-un-AR-doe duh VIN-chee) drew pictures of a helicopter. He never built it. The first helicopter wasn't put together until this century. In 1939, Igor Sikorsky (EE-gore sih-CORE-skee) designed and built the first helicopter that worked.

Leonardo da Vinci's drawing of a helicopter

What is a convertiplane?

Today, the military uses an aircraft called a convertiplane. A convertiplane is a plane that takes off and lands like a helicopter, but flies like a plane when it's in the air. This makes it easy for the plane to land and take off without a runway. Convertiplanes cost more to build than regular airplanes.

51

THE SST

What is a sonic boom?

A sonic boom is the noise made by a supersonic airplane. *Supersonic* means traveling through the air faster than the speed of sound—about 1,100 feet per second. When a plane is flying, waves of air build up in front of it. When a plane flies faster than the speed of sound, the waves become cone-shaped. The plane is inside the tip of the cone. A cone-shaped air wave is called a shock wave. When the cone sweeps over the ground, it makes a loud noise called a sonic boom. Over a period of time, such loud noises can damage ears.

A sonic boom can break windows and crack walls!

What is the SST?

SST stands for supersonic transport. SSTs fly faster than the speed of sound. Most planes don't fly nearly that fast. The Russian Tu-144 and the French and British Concordes are supersonic planes. The Concorde flies at about 1,019 miles an hour. A Boeing 747, which is not supersonic, flies at about 595 miles an hour.

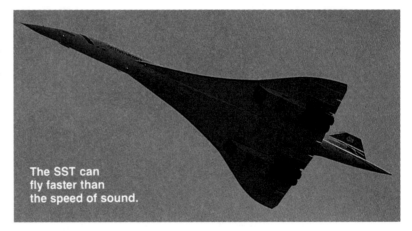

The SST can fly faster than the speed of sound.

What does the SST look like?

The SST is shaped like a dart. The wings are thin and swept back. When planes fly at supersonic speeds, air pressure against the fast-moving plane becomes very strong. The SST's nose comes to a sharp point so that the plane can cut through the hard pressure of the air. The body of the plane is only 9 feet 5 inches wide. This narrowness helps the plane cut through the air quickly. The SST has specially designed wings called deltas. These wings help the SST reach its supersonic speeds.

SEAPLANES AND AMPHIBIANS

Special floats on a seaplane enable it to land on water.

What is a seaplane?

A seaplane is an airplane that can land and take off on water. Under its body, a seaplane has long, tube-shaped floats instead of wheels.

Can a seaplane land on the ground?

No, but there are planes called amphibians (am-FIB-ee-uns) that can. An amphibian is a seaplane that has wheels that can be lowered for a ground landing. This plane was named after the animals known as amphibians. Frogs, toads, and salamanders are all amphibians. They live part of their lives in water and part on land.

WELL, I SEE YOU'RE READY TO LAND ON EITHER THE GROUND OR THE WATER!

GLIDERS

What is a glider?

A glider is an airplane without an engine. It is usually towed up into the air by an engine-powered airplane. The two are connected by a tow rope. When the rope is released, the glider flies through currents of rising air called "updrafts." The air pushes the glider up. When there is no wind, the glider lands.

Strapped into his harness, this hang glider pilot floats through the air.

What is hang gliding?

Hang gliding is a popular American sport. The person gliding wears a harness attached to a glider. The glider looks like a huge triangular kite. Its widest point is about twice as long as a car. There is a control bar so that the pilot can steer.

WHAT'S THAT IN THE SKY?

IS IT A BIRD?

HANG GLIDING LESSONS TODAY

How does a hang glider work?

The pilot usually holds on to the glider and races down a hill into the wind. A more experienced pilot might jump off a cliff. The wind lifts the glider into the air. A hang glider can travel about the speed of a car on a busy street. A person learning to hang glide usually flies about as high as a house. After a while, an experienced pilot may take the glider up higher.

A parasailor gets help from the wind and a power boat.

IS IT A PLANE?

NO. IT'S SUPER WOODSTOCK!

Which sport combines sea and air power?

The sport of parasailing, made popular in Hawaii, combines aspects of hang gliding and water skiing into a fun air sport. The parasailor rides a parachute that is pulled by a motorboat and lifted into the air. The parasail is attached to the motorboat with a strong cable that is controlled by people in the boat. On some boats, the cable can be as long as 600 feet, giving you the same view you'd get from a 60-story building.

PLANES WITHOUT WINGS OR TAILS!

HEY, WHERE ARE THE WINGS?

How does a plane without wings fly?

The HL-10 is a wingless plane. It flies by rocket power. It travels at a speed of 610 miles per hour as it climbs into the air. When it reaches its flying height, the HL-10 moves forward at 1,200 miles per hour—faster than a supersonic plane.

What plane flies without a tail?

A plane called the Northrop Flying Wing, first built in the 1940s, had no tail. It didn't have a body, either. It was just two big wings put together. The pilot and crew sat in the cockpit located at the point where the two wings met. The tips of the wings were swept back. The plane was very thick in the middle. Some models reached speeds of 200 miles an hour!

It's not a big bird—it's the flying wing!

In 1959, French inventors flew a Coleopter, an amazing wingless craft that looked just like a flying saucer!

VULCAN AND VOYAGER

What other unusually shaped planes are there?

The Avro Vulcan, first flown in August, 1952, is a plane that looks a bit odd. It's a big triangle. The wings form two points of the triangle, and the nose forms the third point. In most planes, the tail assembly is behind the wings. In the Avro Vulcan, it lines up with the wings.

The Vulcan is 111 feet wide and 97 feet long. It was used as a bomber and had a crew of five.

THE VOYAGER

What is the Voyager plane?

The Voyager is a plane that was built by two pilots, Dick Rutan and Jeana Yeager, who believed it was possible to fly around the world without refueling. Specially designed to save fuel, the *Voyager* has a huge wingspan of 110 feet, flexible wings that can move 30 feet up and down, and 17 fuel tanks. These design features allowed the two pilots to circle the world in nine days, in December of 1986, without ever once touching down.

SUPER FLIERS OF THE FUTURE

What is the Hypersonic transport?

The Hypersonic transport is a plane being built by both the U.S. government and private aircraft makers. When completed, the Hypersonic is expected to reach speeds of up to Mach 25, 25 times the speed of sound. In comparison, the SST flies at *only* Mach 2.2. Other nations, including France and England, are working on similar superfast planes.

Hypersonic
Transport

Will everyone own planes in the future?

No one knows for sure what the future will bring, but there's a good chance that many people will use planes instead of cars. These planes will have to lift off like helicopters because there isn't enough room on Earth for everyone to have a private runway.

Have any planes for individual use been invented?

A scientist named Paul Moller has developed a plane called the Moller Merlin 200. It can rise straight up in the air and can go about 400 miles per hour. Its inventor claims that it can even take off from water.

The Merlin 200 can be filled up at an ordinary gas station!

59

DID YOU KNOW...?

Skydivers form a star pattern.

● Skydiving is a popular modern sport. Skydivers jump out of airplanes and do stunts in the sky. They do loops, turns, barrel rolls, and more. Sometimes a group of skydivers will hold hands and form a ring.

When skydivers get close to the ground, they open their parachutes to slow down their fall. Before skydivers open their parachutes, they can float through the air at 200 miles an hour! That's nearly four times as fast as a car on a highway!

● Many people have managed to swim across the English Channel, but Bryan Allen was the first person to pedal across in an airplane! He did it in a human-powered airplane called the *Gossamer Albatross*. It was made of plastic and piano wire. In June 1979, Bryan made the 23-mile channel trip.

On April 23, 1988, another pilot flew from Crete to mainland Greece in a pedal plane. The pilot was a Greek cycling champ named Kanellos Kanellopoulos. He covered 74 miles in his trip across the Aegean Sea.

● A big airplane may use more than 300,000 pounds of fuel on a long flight. That much fuel could fill a midsized swimming pool!

SNOOPY FOR PRESIDENT...

- Some planes can write messages in the sky. These planes carry a tank that holds a mixture of chlorine gas and the chemical element titanium. This mixture makes smoke, which the pilot turns into puffy white letters in the sky.

- Every year at Wittman Airfield in Oshkosh, Wisconsin, pilots from all over the world attend the Experimental Aircraft Association Fly-In Convention. It is the world's largest flying event. Nearly 15,000 aircraft and one million people attend. Many of these airplanes have been built by their owners. For eight days, Wittman Airfield becomes the busiest airport in the world.

- Air Force One is the radio code for any plane that carries the President of the United States. There are two planes that have been specially made for the President and his staff, but these two planes are getting old and will soon be replaced.

The new Air Force One jets will be able to fly 6,900 miles without refueling. They will have crews of 23 and will be able to carry 80 passengers. Each new plane will have an office, a conference room, and a bedroom for the President. On board each plane will be a small hospital and two kitchens that can carry enough food to feed 100 people for up to a week.

I KNOW IT'S NOT AS GOOD AS THE FOOD ON AIR FORCE ONE, BUT...